NINJA FOODI DIGITAL AIR FRYER OVEN COOKBOOK 1000

The Complete Ninja Air Fryer Oven Recipe Book|1000-Day Easy Quick Tasty Dishes| Air Fry, Roast, Broil, Bake, Bagel, Toast, Dehydrate and More

By Dr. Jim Abaden

Warning-Disclaimer
The purpose of this book is to educate and entertain. The author or publisher does not guarantee that anyone following the techniques, suggestions, tips, ideas, or strategies will become successful. The author and publisher shall have neither liability or responsibility to anyone with respect to any loss or damage caused, or alleged to be caused, directly or indirectly by the information contained in this book.

Table of Contents

Description...1

Introduction..2

   What Is the Ninja Foodi Air Fryer Oven?................................... 2

   Tips for usage, Cleaning & Maintenance....................................5

   Matters Need Attention...6

CHAPTER 1: BRUNCHES..7

   Coconut-Blueberry Cereal..7

   Air-Fried Omelet..8

   Sunny Side up Egg Tarts.. 9

   Air Toasted Cheese Sandwich.. 10

   Crunchy Zucchini Hash Browns..11

   Air Toasted French Toast...12

   Citrus Blueberry Breakfast Muffins.. 13

   Peanut Butter and Jelly Breakfast Donuts.............................. 14

CHAPTER 2: BEEF, PORK, & LAMB...16

   Air Roasted Steak..16

   Air Roasted Pork Ribs..17

   Air Roasted Lamb..19

   Asian Air Broiled Pork Chops..20

   Air fried Bacon... 22

   Italian Pork Milanese..23

   Air Roasted Jerk Pork...25

   Air Fryer Baked Meatloaf..26

   Air Fried Steak... 28

CHAPTER 3: FISH & SEAFOOD..30

   Air Broiled Mahi Mahi Tacos...30

   Crispy Air Fried Cod..32

Air Roasted Tilapia..33
Baked Salmon...34
Air Fried Shrimp..35
Air Fried Catfish...36
Baked Coconut Shrimp..37
Air Broiled Lemon Tilapia...39

CHAPTER 4: CHICKEN & POULTRY...40

Air Fried Chili Chicken...40
Air Roasted Turkey..41
Air-Fried Lemon Chicken...42
Baked Chicken Thighs..43
Turkey Wraps with Sauce...44
Air Roasted Chicken Drumsticks..46
Scrumptious Turkey Wraps..47
Air Roasted Whole Chicken...48

CHAPTER 5: VEGAN & VEGETARIAN......................................50

Air Fried Vegetables..50
Air Broiled Mushrooms...51
Hydrated Potato Wedges..52
Crispy Baked Tofu...53
Spiced Tempeh...54
Steamed Broccoli..56
Air Fried Brussel Sprouts...57
Hydrated Kale Chips...58

CHAPTER 6: SOUPS, STEWS & BROTHS................................59

Chicken and Veggie Soup...59
Air Roasted Roots Soup..60

CHAPTER 7: DESSERTS AND SNACKS...................................61

Air Baked Cheesecake..61
Air Roasted Nuts..63

Air Fried White Corn...64
Fruit Cake..65
Hydrated Apples...66
Nutty Slice..67
<u>Energy Brownies</u>..68
Air Fry Toaster Oven Bars...69

CHAPTER 8: BEANS AND EGGS..**70**

Air Fried Beans..70
Egg and Spinach Scramble..71
Hydrated Green Beans...72
Egg and Mushroom Frittata...73
Air Baked Omelet...74
Air Fryer Cooked Bean Dish...75
Bacon Omelet...76
Air Fryer Baked Beans...77

Conclusion..**78**

Description

When it comes to cooking, we all have one desire, well two three:

1. To have an easy cooking experience that doesn't involve a whole bunch of dirty utensils
2. To cut down the amount of time we spend cooking, and
3. To have the tastiest meal waiting for us at the end of the cooking process.

Consider the Ninja Foodi Digital Air Fryer Oven Cookbook your kitchen genie as it's going to provide you with the above mentioned desires and so much more. Imagine one appliance that allows you eight different functions! From the air broil, air roast, air fry, bake, toast, bagel, keep warm and dehydrate, you are going to have one of your best cooking experiences with the Ninja Foodi Digital Air Fryer Oven Cookbook!

Introduction

The holiday season is right around the corner and for most families this is a period where the most delicious recipes that have been carried on from generation to generation are cooked. We are talking about soulful stews and soups, deliciously marinated grills and the sweetest and most aromatic baked foods.

To prepare such a buffet for your family and loved ones, you need to be well equipped with the right appliances for you to cook up a storm without getting overwhelmed and without the risk of making underwhelming food. Your reputation depends on it and the last thing you want is to be known as the person who ruined Christmas dinner experience for everyone.

You'll therefore need the perfect cooking partner that can help you cook 8 different meals without breaking sweat and this is non-other than the Ninja Foodi Digital Air Fryer Oven.

Aren't all air fryers the same?

No! As you are going to discover in this book. We are going to take an in-depth look at the Ninja Foodi Digital Air Fryer Oven Cookbook. Its features and functionality. How to use it and why you need to bring it to your kitchen. We also have the simplest and tastiest recipes that will help you turn you into quite the master chef without sweating yourself crazy in the kitchen.

Without further ado, let's get more information on the Ninja Foodi Digital Air Fryer Oven Cookbook.

What Is the Ninja Foodi Digital Air Fryer Oven?

The Ninja Foodi Digital Air Fryer Oven is built on the raving reviews of the other Ninja Foodi kitchen appliances. Just as the name suggests, it is a beautiful combination of an air fryer and a toaster oven in a neat and portable package that doesn't take up much of your kitchen space.

The question you are probably asking yourself is, if it is a worthy investment especially if you already have an air fryer or a toaster oven.

Well here are some of its features that will help you make a decision:

Appearance

If you like your kitchen with exquisite and immaculate appliances, then the Ninja Foodi Air Fryer Oven is definitely for you. It's made from polished stainless steel giving it an expensive glossy look. It also has rounded edges that minimize contact injuries and it has a digital control pad that makes it so easy to choose the cooking style that you are going for.

In terms of size, it is slightly shorter and wider than the average toaster oven. Another impressive attribute of the Ninja Foodi Air Fryer Oven is that when it is not in use and is completely cool, you can flip it to vertical position and set it in a corner to create more space on your counter.

It also comes with a sturdy air fryer basket, a crumb tray, non-stick sheet pan and a cooking rack. The great thing is that these add-ons are larger than what you would have in a toaster oven since it's wider. This gives you the ability to make more food.

Functionality

You can already tell from the name that the Ninja Foodi Digital Air Fryer Oven air fries and toasts food. In addition to these functions, it also air broils, air fries, bakes, keeps food warm and dehydrates food. You can also use it to make bagels. Talk about a miracle worker in your kitchen!

a. Air Fry

If you are looking for crisp, flavorful and healthy air fried meals, then the Ninja Foodi Digital Air Fryer is exactly what you need. Whether you are frying chicken or fries, you will get that beautiful crisp and golden finish with very little amount of oil used. Recreate your favorite fried take-out with the air fryer function.

b. Air roast

This function works perfectly for sheet pan meals such as a combination of a protein like seafood, steak or chicken; veggies like potatoes, broccoli or asparagus and your choice of herbs and spices. One thing that's going to blow your socks off is how quick your dinner is going to be and how tender and beautiful browned it's going to be.

c. Toast

This air fryer oven allows for up to 9 slices of bread laid out without squeezing them and unlike most toaster ovens, the end result is perfectly evenly browned slices.

d. Bagel

This is a similar function to toast only that instead of slices of bread, you use bagel halves which come out pretty even with a nice crisp and golden finish.

e. Air broil

The fact that the Ninja Foodi Digital Air Fryer Oven is fact allows for juicy chicken and steak with a beautiful brown finish.

f. Bake

For the best baking results, make muffins, biscuits or buns or small loaves of bread as a large loaf pan or bundt pan will not fit well. It's very easy to use and some of our recipes will give you the best tutorial on how to use this air fryer oven.

g. Dehydrate

One feature you are truly going to enjoy with the Ninja Foodi Digital Air Fryer Oven is its large size compared to most air fryer toaster ovens. This means it can be able to accommodate more food that you want to dehydrate such as banana slice or tarro slices. Enjoy some peace and quiet as you go about your business without the interference of the air fryer oven as it dehydrates your food.

h. Keep warm

This air fryer oven can keep your food warm for up to 2 hours. As a rule of thumb, cover your food to avoid t drying out.

Tips for usage, Cleaning & Maintenance

The Ninja Foodi Digital Air Fryer Oven has a digital control panel that is so simple to read and that is very well laid out. It also has a knob that you will use to set the temperature, time, level of doneness and also number of slices you want to toast for example.

One very useful feature is the fact that the oven automatically preheats itself and it only takes one minute to do so thus saving on your cook time. You can also turn on the light on the interior to keep tabs on your food.

Cleaning

Cleaning is pretty simple and straightforward. The air frying basket is dishwasher safe. As for the oven, put it in vertical position and you can easily open the posterior side allowing to easily clean the inside.

The oven should be cleaned after use at all times. Start by unplugging and allowing it to cool down completely then empty the crumb tray.

Use a soft damp cloth with dish soap to clean the interior and exterior surfaces.

For deep cleansing, remove all detachable accessories and attachments and wash them separately with warm water, dish soap and a soft brush or sponge.

Gently open the back door and wipe the interiors using a sponge with dish soap and wipe clean with a damp towel. Never place the oven in a dish washer or in a large basin of water.

Maintenance

Maintenance is pretty simple when you follow the cleaning guidelines and the matters that need attention below. Always store the oven away from heat and in a stable surface. If you notice any problem with your Ninja Foodi Digital Air Fryer Oven, contact the Shark Ninja team as they understand the product and will give you the help you need.

Keep your oven and all its accessories clean and well stored, follow the user manual and you are going to enjoy a long lasting relationship.

Matters Need Attention

1. Always keep an eye on the oven whilst in use.
2. Don't use kitchen foil to cover the broil pan, sheet pan, crumb tray or any part of the oven as this could cause it to overheat which could easily lead to a fire.
3. Don't put more food in the oven than can be accommodated. When food gets in contact with the heating elements as this could damage the oven or result in injury.
4. To prevent accidents, do not touch the oven when in use without protective gloves. The oven actually stays hot after cooking so handle it carefully to avoid accidents.
5. When cleaning, don't use metallic scrubbing pads as small pieces can get in contact with the electrical elements thus posing the risk of electric shock.
6. Unplug the oven when it's not in use to avoid falling down by accident.
7. When using the oven, ensure it is not near any flammable materials such as drapes or kitchen towels to avoid risk of a fire breakout.
8. Do not use any attachments or oven accessories that are not provided by Shark Ninja as it could lead to your oven malfunctioning.
9. Only use the oven to serve the purpose it was used to avoid malfunctions.
10. When using cooking equipment that is not made of oven friendly glass or metal, pay close attention to avoid accidents.

CHAPTER 1: BRUNCHES

Coconut-Blueberry Cereal

Prep Time: 20 minutes/ Cook Time 20 minutes/ Serves: 4

Ingredients

- 1/2 cup dried blueberries
- 1/2 cup unsweetened coconut flakes
- 1 cup pumpkin seeds
- 2 cups chopped pecans
- 6 medium dates, pitted
- 1/3 cup coconut oil
- 2 tsp. cinnamon
- 1/2 tsp. sea salt

Directions

1. Add coconut oil, dates and half the pecans to a food processor; pulse until finely ground.
2. Add pumpkin seeds and the remaining pecans and continue pulsing until roughly chopped.
3. Transfer the mixture to a large bowl and add cinnamon, vanilla and salt; spread on a baking sheet/ pan that can fit in your foodi air fry toaster oven and set on bake at 325 degrees for about 20 minutes or until browned.
4. Remove from the foodi air fry toaster oven and let cool slightly before stirring in blueberries and coconut.
5. Enjoy!

Nutrition value per serving:

Calories: 372 kcal, Carbs: 12 g, Fat: 25.2 g, Protein: 20.1 g.

Air-Fried Omelet

Prep Time: 10 minutes/ Cook Time 10 minutes/ Serves: 2

Ingredients

- 3 large eggs
- 100g ham, cut into small pieces
- 1/4 cup milk
- 3/4 cup mixed vegetables (mushrooms, scallions, bell pepper)
- 1/4 cup mixed cheddar and mozzarella cheese
- 1 tsp. mixed herbs
- Salt and freshly ground pepper to taste

Directions

1. Combine the eggs and milk in a medium bowl then add in the remaining ingredients apart from the cheese and mixed herbs and beat well using a fork.
2. Pour the egg mix into an evenly greased pan then place it in the basket of your air fry toaster oven.
3. Set on bake for 350 degrees for 10 minutes.
4. Sprinkle the cheese and mixed herbs on the omelet halfway through cook time.
5. Gently loosen the omelet from the sides of the pan using a spatula.
6. Serve hot!

Nutrition value per serving:

Calories: 278 kcal, Carbs: 1.3 g, Fat: 4.6 g, Protein: 24.1 g.

Sunny Side up Egg Tarts

Prep Time: 15 minutes/ Cook Time 20 minutes/ Serves: 2

Ingredients

- 4 eggs
- 3/4 cup shredded Gruyere cheese (or preferred cheese)
- 1 sheet of puff pastry
- Minced chives for topping

Directions

1. Start by flouring a clean surface then gently roll out your sheet of puff pastry and divide it into four equal squares.
2. If you have a small air fryer toast oven, start with two squares but if it's big enough, go ahead and place the squares on the basket and cook for about 8-10 minutes or until they turn golden brown.
3. Whilst still in the basket, gently make an indentation at the center of each square and sprinkle 2-4 tablespoons of shredded cheese in the well then crack an egg on top.
4. Cook for 5-10 minutes or to desired doneness.
5. Remove from air fryer toast oven, sprinkle with chives and you are ready to eat!

Nutrition value per serving:

Calories: 403 kcal, Carbs: 10.8 g, Fat: 29.4 g, Protein: 24.6 g.

Air Toasted Cheese Sandwich

Prep Time: 15 minutes/ Cook Time 20 minutes/ Serves: 2

Ingredients

- 2 eggs
- 4 slices of bread of choice
- 4 slices turkey
- 4 slices ham
- 6 tbsp. half and half cream
- 2 tsp. melted butter
- 4 slices Swiss cheese
- 1/4 tsp. pure vanilla extract
- Powdered sugar and raspberry jam for serving

Directions

1. Mix the eggs, vanilla and cream in a bowl and set aside.
2. Make a sandwich with the bread layered with cheese slice, turkey, ham, cheese slice and the top slice of bread to make two sandwiches. Gently press on the sandwiches to somewhat flatten them.
3. Spread out kitchen aluminum foil and cut it about the same size as the sandwich and spread the melted butter on the surface of the foil.
4. Dip the sandwich in the egg mixture and let it soak for about 20 seconds on each side. Repeat this for the other sandwich. Place the soaked sandwiches on the prepared foil sheets then place on the basket in your fryer.
5. Set on toast and cook for 12 minutes then flip the sandwiches and brush with the remaining butter and cook for another 5 minutes or until well browned.
6. Place the cooked sandwiched on a plate and top with the powdered sugar and serve with a small bowl of raspberry jam.
7. Enjoy!

Nutrition value per serving:

Calories: 735 kcal, Carbs: 13.4 g, Fat: 47.9 g, Protein: 40.8 g.

Crunchy Zucchini Hash Browns

Prep Time: 30 minutes/ Cook Time 15 minutes/ Serves: 3

Ingredients

- 4 medium zucchini, peeled and grated
- 1 tsp. onion powder
- 1 tsp. garlic powder
- 2 tbsp. almond flour
- 1-1/2 tsp. chili flakes
- Salt and freshly ground pepper to taste
- 2 tsp. olive oil

Directions

1. Put the grated zucchini in between layers of kitchen towel and squeeze to drain excess water. Pour 1 teaspoon of oil in a pan, preferably non-stick, over medium heat and sauté the potatoes for about 3 minutes.
2. Transfer the zucchini to a shallow bowl and let cool. Sprinkle the zucchini with the remaining ingredients and mix until well combined.
3. Transfer the zucchini mix to a flat plate and pat it down to make 1 compact layer. Put in the fridge and let it sit for 20 minutes.
4. Set your air fryer toast oven to 360 degrees F.
5. Meanwhile take out the flattened zucchini and divide into equal portions using a knife or cookie cutter.
6. Lightly brush your air fryer toast oven's basket with the remaining teaspoon of olive oil.
7. Gently place the zucchini pieces into the greased basket and fry for 12-15 minutes, flipping the hash browns halfway through.
8. Enjoy hot!

Nutrition value per serving:

Calories: 195 kcal, Carbs: 10.4 g, Fat: 13.1 g, Protein: 9.6 g.

Air Toasted French Toast

Prep Time: 5 minutes/ Cook Time 20 minutes/ Serves: 3

Ingredients

- 6 slices of preferred bread
- 3/4 cup of milk
- 3 eggs
- 1 tsp. pure vanilla extract
- 1 tbsp. ground cinnamon

Directions

1. Combine all the ingredients apart from the bread in a medium bowl until well mixed.
2. Dunk each slice of bread into the egg mix, gently shake the excess off and place in a greased pan.
3. Air toast in the fryer, for 6 minutes.
4. To serve, drizzle with maple syrup.

Nutrition value per serving:

Calories: 245 kcal, Carbs: 28.5 g, Fat: 7.5 g, Protein: 14.9 g.

Citrus Blueberry Breakfast Muffins

Prep Time: 15 minutes/ Cook Time 15 minutes/ Serves: 3-4

Ingredients

- 2-1/2 cups cake flour
- 1/2 cup sugar
- 1/4 cup light cooking oil such as avocado oil
- 1/2 cup heavy cream
- 1 cup fresh blueberries
- 2 eggs
- Zest and juice from 1 orange
- 1 tsp. pure vanilla extract
- 1 tsp. brown sugar for topping

Directions

1. Start by combining the oil, heavy cream, eggs, orange juice and vanilla extract in a large bowl then set aside.
2. Separately combine the flour and sugar until evenly mixed then pour little by little into the wet ingredients.
3. Combine well unlit well blended but careful not to over mix.
4. Preheat your air fryer toast oven at 320 degrees F
5. Gently fold the blueberries into the batter and divide into cupcake holders, preferably, silicone cupcake holders as you won't have to grease them. Alternatively you can use cupcake paper liners on any cupcake holders/ tray you could be having.
6. Sprinkle the tops with the brown sugar and pop the muffins in the fryer.
7. Bake for about 12 minutes. Use a toothpick to check for readiness. When the muffins have evenly browned and an inserted toothpick comes out clean, they are ready.
8. Take out the muffins and let cool.
9. Enjoy!

Nutrition value per serving:

Calories: 289 kcal, Carbs: 12.8 g, Fat: 32 g, Protein: 21.1 g.

Peanut Butter and Jelly Breakfast Donuts

Prep Time: 15 minutes/ Cook Time 12 minutes/ Serves: 4

Ingredients

For the Donuts:

- 1-1/4 cups all-purpose flour
- 1/2 tsp. baking soda
- 1/2 tsp. baking powder
- 1/3 cup sugar
- 1/2 cup buttermilk
- 1 large egg
- 1 tsp. pure vanilla extract
- 3 tbsp. unsalted, melted and divided into 2+1
- 3/4 tsp. salt

For the Glaze:

- 2 tbsp. milk
- 1/2 cup powdered sugar
- 2 tbsp. smooth peanut butter
- Sea salt to taste

For the Filling:

- 1/2 cup strawberry or blueberry jelly

Directions

1. Whisk together all the dry ingredients for the donut in a large bowl.
2. Separately combine the egg, buttermilk, melted butter and vanilla extract.
3. Create a small well at the center of the dry ingredients and pour in the egg mixture. Use a fork to combine the ingredients then finish off with a spatula.
4. Place the dough on a floured surface and knead the dough. It will start out sticky but as you knead, it's going to come together.

5. Roll out the dough to make a 3/4 inch thick circle. Use a cookie cutter, or the top part of a cup to cut the dough into rounds.
6. Place the donuts on a parchment paper and then into your air fryer toast oven. You may have to cook in batches depending on the size of your air fryer toast oven.
7. Set on bagel for 12 minutes at 350 degrees F.
8. Use a pastry bag or squeeze bottle to fill the donuts with jelly.
9. Combine the glaze ingredients and drizzle on top of the donuts.
10. Enjoy!

Nutrition value per serving:

Calories: 430 kcal, Carbs: 66.8 g, Fat: 14.6 g, Protein: 9.1 g.

CHAPTER 2: BEEF, PORK, & LAMB

Air Roasted Steak

Prep Time: 5 minutes/ Cook Time 15 minutes/ Serves: 2

Ingredients

- 2 rib-eye steaks, sliced 1-1/2- inch pieces
- 1/2 cup soy sauce
- 1/4 cup olive oil
- 4 teaspoons grill seasoning

Directions

1. In a resealable bag, combine steaks, seasoning, olive oil and soy sauce; shake to coat well and let marinate for at least 2 hours.
2. Remove the meat from the bag and discard the marinade.
3. Add a splash of water to the air fryer toast oven pan and then preheat to 400 degrees.
4. Add the meat to the basket and air roast for 7 minutes.
5. Turn over the steak and air roast for another 8 minutes.
6. Turn off the air fry oven and let rest for at least 5 minutes before serving.

Nutrition value per serving:

Calories: 652 kcal, Carbs: 7.5 g, Fat: 49.1g, Protein: 44 g.

Air Roasted Pork Ribs

Prep Time: 2-12 hours/ Cook Time 15 minutes/ Serves: 4

Ingredients

- 1 rack pork baby back ribs
- 1 tbsp. oyster sauce
- 2 tbsp. light soy sauce
- 1 tsp. dark soy sauce
- 1 tbsp. mustard
- 1-1/2 tbsp. pure honey
- 5 cloves garlic, halved
- 1 inch fresh garlic, sliced

For the sauce:

- 1 tbsp. soy sauce
- 1 tbsp. fish sauce
- 2 tsp. toasted rice powder
- 1 tsp. sugar
- 2 tsp. red chili flakes
- Freshly squeezed juice of 1/2 a lemon
- 2 tsp. finely chopped cilantro
- 1 clove garlic, finely chopped

Directions

1. Combine all the ingredients for the ribs, apart from the ribs, in a bowl to make the marinade.
2. Separate the ribs and pour the marinade over the ribs in a large bowl ensuring the ribs are well coated. Cover with cling wrap and marinate for a minimum of 2 hours. For best results, marinate overnight.
3. Set your air fry toaster oven to 360 degrees F,
4. Add the ribs, garlic and ginger pieces into the air fryer toast oven. Do not add the juices. Air roast for six minutes, shake well and cook for another 6 minutes.

5. As the ribs are cooking, make the dip by combining all the sauce ingredients then set aside in a small bowl.
6. Serve the ribs hot with the dipping sauce.
7. Enjoy!

Nutrition value per serving:

Calories: 456 kcal, Carbs: 19.7 g, Fat: 15.2 g, Protein: 26.3 g.

Air Roasted Lamb

Prep Time: 5 minutes/ Cook Time 1 hour/ Serves: 4

Ingredients

- 1-1/4 kg Leg of Lamb
- 1 tablespoon olive oil
- A pinch of sea salt
- Pepper

Directions

1. Season the leg of lamb with salt and pepper and place it in the fryer basket.
2. Air roast for 20 minutes at 360 degrees, turn the leg of lamb over and continue roasted for another 20 minutes.
3. Serve with roasted potatoes.

Nutrition value per serving:

Calories: 639 kcal, Carbs: 10.8 g, Fat: 22.6 g, Protein: 102.6 g.

Asian Air Broiled Pork Chops

Prep Time: 15 minutes/ Cook Time 20 minutes/ Serves: 4

Ingredients

- 450g pork chops
- 3/4 cup corn/potato starch
- 1 egg white
- 1/4 tsp. freshly ground black pepper
- 1/2 tsp. kosher salt

For the stir fry:

- 2 green onions, sliced
- 2 jalapeno peppers, seeds removed and sliced
- 2 tbsp. peanut oil
- 1/4 tsp. freshly ground pepper and kosher salt to taste

Directions

1. Brush or spray the basket of your air fryer toast oven with oil.
2. Next, whisk the egg, black pepper and salt until it gets frothy. Cut up the pork chops and use a clean kitchen towel to pat the meat dry.
3. Toss the cutlets in the frothy egg mixture until evenly coated. Cover and marinate for 30 minutes.
4. Place the pork chops in a separate bowl and pour in the corn/ potato starch ensuring each culet is thoroughly dredged. Shake off the excess corn/ potato starch and arrange the pork chops on the prepared basket.
5. Set the air fry toaster oven on air roast at 360 degrees F and cook for 9 minutes, shaking the basket after every 2-3 minutes and spraying or brushing the cutlets with more oil if needed.
6. Turn to broil and cook for 6 more minutes or until the chops are crisp and done to desire.
7. Heat a wok or pan over high heat until extremely hot. Add all the stir fry ingredients and sauté for a minute.

8. Add your cooked pork chops and toss with the stir fry.
9. Cook for another minute ensuring the pork chops are evenly coated with the stir fry ingredients. Enjoy!

Nutrition value per serving:

Calories: 398 kcal, Carbs: 16.1 g, Fat: 17.5 g, Protein: 21.1 g.

Air fried Bacon

Prep Time: 5 minutes/ Cook Time 15 minutes/ Serves: 6

Ingredients

- 1/2 package (16 ounce) bacon

Directions

1. Preheat your air fryer toast oven to 390° F.
2. Arrange the bacon in a single layer in the fryer basket and cook for 8 minutes.
3. Flip over the bacon and cook for 7 minutes more or until crisp.
4. Transfer to a paper lined plate to drain excess grease.
5. Enjoy warm!

Nutrition value per serving:

Calories: 173 kcal, Carbs: 0.2 g, Fat: 17 g, Protein: 4.4 g.

Italian Pork Milanese

Prep Time: 20 minutes/ Cook Time 10 minutes/ Serves: 46

Ingredients

- 6 pork chops, center cut
- 2 eggs
- 2 tbsp. water
- 1 cup panko bread crumbs seasoned with salt and black pepper
- 1/2 cup all-purpose flour
- Parmesan cheese, for serving (optional)
- 2 tbsp. extra virgin olive oil

For arugula salad:

- 1 bag fresh arugula
- 2 tbsp. freshly squeezed lemon juice
- 1 tsp. Dijon mustard
- 1/8 cup extra virgin olive oil
- Freshly ground black pepper and sea salt to taste

Directions

1. Use a mallet or rolling pin to pound each pork chop into 1/4 inch cutlets.
2. Season well with salt and pepper then dip each cutlet in the flour. Shake off the excess.
3. Whisk the eggs with the water in a shallow bowl and dip the floured cutlets in the mixture then roll in the bread crumbs.
4. Do this for all the chops and set aside.
5. Set your air fryer toast oven at 380 degrees F.
6. Lightly brush the breaded pork chops with olive and arrange in one layer on your air fryer toast oven's basket. Cook for 3-5 minutes then flip the chops and cook for another 3-5 minutes or until golden and crisp.
7. Meanwhile, prepare the salad by combining the mustard, lemon juice,

salt and pepper in a large bowl. Toss the arugula with the vinaigrette until evenly coated.

8. Serve the arugula salad and top with crisp cutlets and parmesan cheese (optional). Enjoy!

Nutrition value per serving:

Calories: 417 kcal, Carbs: 23.8 g, Fat: 21.3 g, Protein: 20.1 g.

Air Roasted Jerk Pork

Prep Time: 10 minutes/ Cook Time 1 hour 10 minutes/ Serves: 10

Ingredients

- 1800g pork shoulder
- 1 tbsp. olive oil
- 1/4 cup Jamaican Jerk spice blend
- 1/2 cup beef broth

Directions

1. Rub the roast with oil and dust with spice blend; set your air fryer toast oven to 400 degrees F and air roast on both sides for 4 minutes on each side in a large pan.
2. Let rest for about 5 minutes before removing from oven.
3. Shred and serve.

Nutrition value per serving:

Calories: 298 kcal, Carbs: 7.4 g, Fat: 21.3 g, Protein: 19.6 g.

Air Fryer Baked Meatloaf

Prep Time: 20 minutes/ Cook Time 20 minutes/ Serves: 4

Ingredients

- 450g lean minced meat
- 250 ml tomato sauce
- 1 small onion, finely chopped
- 1 tsp. minced garlic
- 5 tbsp. ketchup
- 1 tbsp. Worcestershire sauce
- 1/3 cup cornflakes crumbs
- 3 tsp. brown sugar
- 1-1/2 tsp. freshly ground black pepper
- 1-1/2 tsp. sea salt
- 1 tsp. dried basil
- 1/2 tsp. freshly chopped parsley

Directions

1. In a large bowl, combine the minced meat, corn flakes crumbs, chopped onion, garlic, basil, salt, pepper and ¾ of the tomato sauce. Use your hands to mix and ensure all the ingredients are evenly combined.
2. Take your two tiny loaf pans and lightly coat with vegetable oil. Divide the meatloaf mix into the two loaf pans.
3. Set your air fryer toast oven to 360 degrees F.
4. For the glaze, combine the remaining tomato sauce, ketchup, Worcestershire sauce and brown sugar in a bowl. Brush this glaze mixture on the top and sides of your two loaves.
5. Put the too loaf pans in the fryer. Bake for 10 minutes and re-apply the glaze on the top and sides of your meatloaves.
6. Bake for another 10 minutes, applying the glaze twice in between.
7. Remove the two loaf pans and sprinkle with the fresh parsley.

8. Let stand for 3 minutes before removing the loaves from the loaf pans.
9. Serve your perfectly moist and flavorful meatloaf with mashed potatoes and a green salad.
10. Enjoy!

Nutrition value per serving:

Calories: 307 kcal, Carbs: 31.2 g, Fat: 9.1 g, Protein: 25.8 g.

Air Fried Steak

Prep Time: 15 minutes/ Cook Time 20 minutes/ Serves: 2

Ingredients

- 2 x 200g sirloin steaks
- 1 cup panko bread crumbs seasoned with kosher salt and freshly ground pepper
- 1 cup all-purpose flour
- 3 eggs, lightly beaten
- 1 tsp. garlic powder
- 1 tsp. onion powder
- For the sausage gravy:
- 150g ground sausage meat
- 2 cups milk
- 2-1/2 tbsp. flour
- 1 tsp. freshly ground black pepper

Directions

1. Use a mallet or rolling pin to pound the two steaks until 1/2 – 1/4-inch thick.
2. Place the flour, egg and panko in three different shallow bowls.
3. First dredge the steak in the flour, followed by the egg and lastly the bread crumbs then set aside on a plate.
4. Lightly brush the basket of your air fryer toast oven with oil then place the two breaded steaks on the basket.
5. Set the air fryer toast oven to 370 degrees F and air roast the steak for 12 minutes, flipping once halfway through cook time. Air broil for 5 minutes or until golden browned.
6. Meanwhile prepare the gravy by cooking the sausage meat in a pan over medium-low heat until it evenly browns. Drain the excess fat and reserve about a tablespoon or two in the pan.
7. Stir in the flour until well incorporated then pour in the milk, little by

little, stirring all the while.

8. Season with freshly ground pepper and simmer for 3 minutes until the gravy is nice and thick.

9. Serve the steak with the gravy and some creamy mashed potatoes. Yum!

Nutrition value per serving:

Calories: 515 kcal, Carbs: 14.8 g, Fat: 41.7 g, Protein: 32.8 g.

CHAPTER 3: FISH & SEAFOOD

Air Broiled Mahi Mahi Tacos

Prep Time: 30 minutes/ Cook Time 20 minutes/ Serves: 2-3

Ingredients

For the tacos:

- 6 flour tortillas
- 1/2 cup all-purpose flour
- 1/4 cup milk
- 1 egg, lightly beaten
- 3 snapper or mahi mahi fillets
- 1 cup panko bread crumbs
- 1/2 tsp. baking powder
- 1/ tsp. ground cumin
- 1 tsp. red chili powder
- Freshly ground black pepper to taste
- 1 tsp. kosher salt
- 1 tbsp. vegetable oil
- 1 lemon, cut into wedges/ slices

For the Spicy Slaw:

- 4 cups shredded green cabbage
- 2 scallions, chopped
- 1/4 cup grated carrots
- 2 tbsp. sweet rice vinegar
- 1/2 cup mayonnaise
- 2 tbsp. sriracha sauce
- 1-1/2 tsp. sugar
- Kosher salt and freshly ground pepper to taste

Directions

1. Start with the slaw. Mix the vinegar, mayonnaise, sriracha and sugar in a bowl until well blended. Toss in the carrots, cabbage and scallions. Keep tossing until the veggies are evenly coated with the dressing. Sprinkle the slaw with salt and pepper. Cover the bowl with cling wrap and put in the fridge. Next mix the flour, cumin, chili, baking powder, salt and pepper in a bowl. Add in the milk and egg and whisk until you get a smooth batter.
2. Place the panko in a bowl. Next cut the fillets into strips, approximately 1 inch in width. Dip the slices in the batter, shake of the excess batter and gently roll them in the bread crumbs then place on a plate. Set your air fryer toast oven to 400 degrees F.
3. Lightly brush the coated fish slices with oil and arrange them in the basket of your air fryer toast oven. Air broil for 3 minutes then flip the fish slices and broil again for 2-3 minutes or until golden brown.
4. Meanwhile warm the tortillas on a pan over low-medium heat for 2 minutes on each side and keep warm on a hot plate. To make the tacos, place the fish slices on each tortilla and top with the spicy slaw. Squeeze the lemon slice/ wedge over the slaw and enjoy!

Nutrition value per serving:

Calories: 287 kcal, Carbs: 11.9 g, Fat: 27.5 g, Protein: 18.7g.

Crispy Air Fried Cod

Prep Time: 10 minutes/ Cook Time 12 minutes/ Serves: 4

Ingredients

- 2 pieces cod fish
- 5 tbsp. light soy sauce
- 1 tsp. dark soy sauce
- 5 tiny pieces of rock sugar
- 3 tbsp. vegetable oil
- 1 dash of sesame oil
- 5 thin slices of ginger
- 1 cup water
- Sugar to taste
- Salt to taste
- 3 spring onions, sliced (with the white and green parts sliced separately
- Coriander, chopped for garnishing

Directions

1. Thoroughly clean the cod then pat dry using a clean kitchen towel.
2. Season well with sugar, salt and 1 dash of sesame oil in a bowl and let stand for 15 minutes.
3. Set your air fryer toast oven to 350 degrees F and air fry the fish for 12 minutes.
4. Meanwhile, pour the cup of water in a pan and over medium-high heat and bring to a boil and the rock sugar, soy sauces and stir well until all the sugar dissolves.
5. Heat the oil in a pan and cook the white part of the scallions and ginger slices until they start browning.
6. Takeout the cod and place on a serving dish.
7. Garnish and pour the hot ginger oil over the fish and also spoon the cooked sauce over it.
8. Enjoy!

Nutrition value per serving:

Calories: 318 kcal, Carbs: 10.1 g, Fat: 20.6 g, Protein: 16.9 g.

Air Roasted Tilapia

Prep Time: 15 minutes/ Cook Time 8 minutes/ Serves: 4

Ingredients

- 4 (4 ounce) tilapia fillets
- 4 cloves crushed garlic
- 3 tablespoons extra-virgin olive oil
- 1 chopped onion
- 1/4 teaspoon salt

Directions

1. Rub the tilapia fillets with garlic and arrange them on a large plate.
2. Drizzle the fish with olive oil until well coated and top with onion.
3. Refrigerate the fish, covered, for at least 8 hours or overnight to soak in the marinade.
4. When ready, preheat your air fryer toast oven to 350 degrees F.
5. Transfer the fish fillets to the basket of your air fryer toast oven; Reserve the marinade for basting.
6. Air roast for 8 minutes, four minutes per side and baste with the marinade halfway through cook time.
7. Enjoy!

Nutrition value per serving:

Calories: 269 kcal, Carbs: 6.4 g, Fat: 17.8 g, Protein: 14 g.

Baked Salmon

Prep Time: 15 minutes/ Cook Time 6 minutes/ Serves: 4

Ingredients

- 1 tablespoon extra-virgin olive oil
- 6 ounces wild salmon fillets, skinless
- Fennel fronds
- 1 tablespoon chopped parsley
- 1 tablespoon chopped dill
- 1 tablespoon chopped chives
- 1 tablespoon chopped tarragon
- 1 tablespoon chopped basil
- 1 tablespoon chopped shallot
- 1 tablespoon lemon juice

Directions

1. Lightly oil the basket of your air fryer toast oven with olive oil; add salmon and fennel wedges and bake for about 6 minutes at 350 degrees F.
2. In a bowl, combine the chopped herbs, extra virgin olive oil, and shallot and lemon juice; stir until well combined.
3. Season and spoon over cooked fish.
4. Serve with steamed rice or mashed potatoes.
5. Enjoy!

Nutrition value per serving:

Calories: 251 kcal, Carbs: 8.7 g, Fat: 19.4 g, Protein: 17.3 g.

Air Fried Shrimp

Prep Time: 10 minutes/ Cook Time 8 minutes/ Serves: 3-4

Ingredients

For the shrimp:
- 450g shrimp, peeled, deveined and cleaned
- 3/4 cup panko bread crumbs
- 1/2 cup all-purpose flour
- 1 large egg white
- Sea salt and freshly ground pepper to taste
- 1 tsp. sweet paprika
- Chicken seasoning to taste

For the hot and sweet sauce:
- 1/4 cup sweet chili sauce
- 1/3 cup plain yogurt
- 2 tbsp. sriracha
- Olive oil cooking spray

Directions

1. Start by setting your air fryer toast oven to 400 degrees F.
2. Place the egg white in a shallow bowl and beat slightly. Place the bread crumbs and the flour in two separate bowls.
3. Season the shrimp with the paprika, salt, pepper and chicken seasoning then dip in the flour followed by the egg white and lastly the bread crumbs
4. Note: Don't dunk the shrimp in the egg white, rather, lightly coat the floured shrimp with the egg white so most of the flour adheres to the shrimp for a crunchier finish.
5. Lightly spray the coated shrimp with cooking spray and gently arrange on the basket of your air fryer toast oven. Air fry each side for 4 minutes or until golden and crispy.
6. For the hot and sweet sauce, mix all the ingredients in a small bowl. You can either toss the cooked shrimp in the sauce or serve the sauce as a dip. Enjoy!

Nutrition value per serving:

Calories: 302 kcal; Carbs: 13.7 g; Fat: 24.9 g; Protein: 19 g

Air Fried Catfish

Prep Time: 10 minutes/ Cook Time 40 minutes/ Serves: 3

Ingredients

- 3 medium catfish fillets
- 1 tbsp. extra virgin olive oil
- 1/4 cup fish fry seasoning of choice
- 2 tbsp. finely chopped fresh parsley for serving

Directions

1. Start by setting your air fryer toast oven to 400 degrees F.
2. Rinse the fillets under tap water and pat dry using a kitchen towel.
3. In a large Ziploc bag, pour in the fish fry seasoning and add in one fish fillet and shake well to ensure it's coated on all sides the place it on a plate. Do this for the remaining fillets.
4. Gently brush olive on all the seasoned fillets and arrange them on your air fryer toast oven's basket. (Cook in batches if they can't all fit)
5. Air fry for 10 minutes then turn the fillets and continue air frying for an additional 10 minutes or until golden brown.
6. You can broil for a further 3-5 minutes for a crispier crust.
7. Serve hot and sprinkle with the Parsley. Enjoy!

Nutrition value per serving:

Calories: 423 kcal, Carbs: 14.5 g, Fat: 38.4 g, Protein: 30 g.

Baked Coconut Shrimp

Prep Time: 20 minutes/ Cook Time 30 minutes/ Serves: 2-3

Ingredients

For the coconut coated shrimp:
- 8 jumbo shrimp, shelled, deveined and thoroughly cleaned
- 1 can (225g) coconut milk
- 1/2 cup panko bread crumbs
- 1/2 cup sweetened grated coconut
- 1/4 tsp. freshly ground pepper, divided
- 1/2 tsp. cayenne pepper, divided
- 1/2 tsp. sea salt, divided

For the spicy dip:
- 1/2 cup orange marmalade
- 1 tsp. mustard
- 1 tbsp. pure honey
- 1/4 tsp. tabasco or hot sauce of choice

Directions

1. Mix the coconut milk with part of the cayenne, salt and ground pepper in a medium bowl until well blended and set aside.
2. Next, combine the shredded coconut, bread crumbs and the remaining salt, cayenne and ground pepper.
3. Dunk the jumbo shrimp, one at a time, roll in the bread crumb mix then gently place in the basket of your air fryer toast oven. Repeat this process for all your shrimp.
4. Set your air fryer toast oven to 350 degrees F and bake for 20 minutes, turning the shrimp halfway though.
5. Meanwhile, combine all the spicy dip ingredients in a small bowl.
6. Serve hot with the marmalade dip.
7. Enjoy!

Nutrition value per serving:

Calories: 326 kcal, Carbs: 13.3 g, Fat: 24.7 g, Protein: 17 g.

Air Broiled Lemon Tilapia

Prep Time: 15 minutes/ Cook Time 2 hours/ Serves: 6

Ingredients

- 6 tilapia filets
- 1 bundle of asparagus
- 12 tbsp. lemon juice
- Lemon pepper seasoning
- 3 tbsp. melted coconut oil

Directions

1. Divide asparagus into equal amounts per each fillet.
2. Place each fillet in the center of a piece of foil and sprinkle with about 1 tsp. lemon pepper seasoning; drizzle with about 2 tbsp. lemon juice and about 1/2 tbsp. melted coconut oil.
3. Top each filet with the asparagus and fold the foil to form a packet.
4. Repeat with the remaining ingredients and then place the packets in the basket of your air fryer toast oven
5. Set the air fryer toast oven to 350 degrees F and broil for 15 minutes.
6. Serve with mashed potatoes. Enjoy!

Nutrition value per serving:

Calories: 374 kcal, Carbs: 9.4 g, Fat: 28.2 g, Protein: 19.3 g.

CHAPTER 4: CHICKEN & POULTRY

Air Fried Chili Chicken

Prep Time: 25 minutes/ Cook Time 10 minutes/ Serves: 4

Ingredients

- 1/2 tablespoon sesame oil
- 1 tablespoon low-sodium soy sauce
- 1 tablespoon cornstarch
- 450g chicken thighs, skinless, boneless, diced
- 1/2 tablespoon peanut oil
- 1 red onion, chopped
- 1 tablespoon minced fresh ginger
- 2 cups snow peas
- 1 tablespoon chili garlic sauce
- 1 mango, peeled, chopped
- 1/8 teaspoon sea salt
- 1/8 teaspoon black pepper

Directions

1. In a large mixing bowl, combine sesame oil, soy sauce, cornstarch and chicken; let sit for at least 20 minutes.
2. In the pan from your air fryer toast oven, heat peanut oil and then sauté ginger and onion for about 2 minutes; add snow peas and stir fry for about 1 minute.
3. Add chicken with the marinade and transfer to your air fryer toast oven and air fry for 5 minutes at 350 degrees F or until chicken is browned.
4. Add chili sauce, mango and pepper and continue stir frying for 1 minute or until chicken is cooked through and mango is tender. Serve the stir fry over cooked brown rice.

Nutrition value per serving:

Calories: 330 kcal, Carbs: 11.8 g, Fat: 24.1 g, Protein: 26 g.

Air Roasted Turkey

Prep Time: 10 minutes/ Cook Time 40 minutes/ Serves: 6

Ingredients

- 2-3/4 pounds turkey breast
- 2 tablespoons unsalted butter
- 1 tablespoon chopped fresh rosemary
- 1 teaspoon chopped fresh chives
- 1 teaspoon minced fresh garlic
- 1/4 teaspoon black pepper
- 1/2 teaspoon salt

Directions

1. Preheat your air fryer toast oven to 350° F.
2. In a bowl, mix together chives, rosemary, garlic, salt and pepper until well combined. Cut in butter and mash until well blended.
3. Rub the turkey breast with the herbed butter and then add to the air fryer toast oven basket; air roast for 20 minutes.
4. Turn the turkey breast and air roast for another 20 minutes.
5. Transfer the cooked turkey onto an aluminum foil and wrap; let rest for at least 10 minutes and then slice it up. Serve warm.

Nutrition value per serving:

Calories: 263 kcal, Carbs: 0.3 g, Fat: 10.1 g, Protein: 40.2 g.

Air-Fried Lemon Chicken

Prep Time: 10 minutes/ Cook Time 15 minutes/ Serves: 4

Ingredients

- 4 Boneless Skinless Chicken Breasts
- 1/2teaspoon organic cumin
- 1teaspoon sea salt (real salt)
- 1/4teaspoon black pepper
- 1/2cup butter, melted
- 1 lemons1/2 juiced, 1/2 thinly sliced
- 1cup chicken bone-broth
- 1can pitted green olives
- 1/2cup red onions, sliced

Directions

1. Liberally season the chicken breasts with sea salt, cumin and black pepper
2. Preheat your air fryer toast oven to 370 degrees and brush the chicken breasts with the melted butter.
3. Air fry in the pan of your air fry toaster oven for about 5 minutes until evenly browned.
4. Add all remaining ingredients and air broil for 10 minutes.
5. Serve hot!

Nutrition value per serving:

Calories: 310 kcal, Carbs: 10.2 g, Fat: 9.4 g, Protein: 21.8 g.

Baked Chicken Thighs

Prep Time: 15 minutes/ Cook Time 35 minutes/ Serves: 4

Ingredients

- 500g chicken thighs
- 1 teaspoon red pepper flakes
- 1 teaspoon sweet paprika
- 1 teaspoon freshly ground black pepper
- 1 teaspoon dried oregano
- 1 teaspoon curry powder
- 1 tablespoon garlic powder
- 1-2 tablespoons coconut oil

Directions

1. Start by preheating your air fryer toast oven to 370 degrees F and preparing the basket of the fryer by lining it with parchment paper.
2. Combine all the spices in a small bowl then set aside.
3. Now arrange the thighs on your prepared basket with the skin side down (remember to first pat the skin dry with kitchen towels).
4. Sprinkle the upper side of the chicken thighs with half the seasoning mix, flip them over and sprinkle the lower side with the remaining seasoning mix.
5. Bake for about 30 minutes until the chicken thighs are cooked through and the skin is crisp.
6. Turn once half way through cook time.
7. To make the skin crispier, increase the heat to 400 degrees and bake for 5 more minutes.
8. Enjoy!

Nutrition value per serving:

Calories: 281 kcal, Carbs: 3 g, Fat: 13 g, Protein: 36.8 g.

Turkey Wraps with Sauce

Prep Time: 10 minutes/ Cook Time 16 minutes/ Serves: 6

Ingredients

Wraps

- 4 large collard leaves, stems removed
- 1 medium avocado, sliced
- 1/2 cucumber, thinly sliced
- 1 cup diced mango
- 6 large strawberries, thinly sliced
- 6 (200g) grilled turkey breasts, diced
- 24 mint leaves

Dipping Sauce

- 2 tablespoons almond butter
- 2 tablespoons coconut cream
- 1 birds eye chili, finely chopped
- 2 tablespoons unsweetened applesauce
- 1/4 cup fresh lime juice
- 1 teaspoon sesame oil
- 1 tablespoon apple cider vinegar
- 1 tablespoon tahini
- 1 clove garlic, crushed
- 1 tablespoon grated fresh ginger
- 1/8 teaspoon sea salt

Directions

For the chicken breasts:

1. Start by setting your air fryer toast oven to 350 degrees F.
2. Lightly coat the basket of the air fryer toast oven with oil.
3. Season the turkey with salt and pepper and arrange on the prepared basket and air fry for 8 minutes on each side.

4. Once done, remove from air fryer toast oven and set on a platter to cool slightly then dice them up.

For the wraps:

5. Divide the veggies and diced turkey breasts equally among the four large collard leaves; fold bottom edges over the filling, and then both sides and roll very tightly up to the end of the leaves; secure with toothpicks and cut each in half.

Make the sauce:

6. Combine all the sauce ingredients in a blender and blend until very smooth. Divide between bowls and serve with the wraps.

Nutrition value per serving:

Calories: 389 kcal, Carbs: 11.7 g, Fat: 38.2 g, Protein: 26 g.

Air Roasted Chicken Drumsticks

Prep Time: 10 minutes/ Cook Time 20 minutes/ Serves: 4

Ingredients

- 1 tbsp. olive oil
- 1-1/2 red onions, diced
- 1-1/2 teaspoons salt
- 8 chicken drumsticks
- 1/2 teaspoon pepper
- 1/4 teaspoon chili powder
- 2 tablespoons thyme leaves
- Zest of 1/4 lemon
- 8 cloves of garlic
- 2/3 cup diced tinned tomatoes
- 2 tbsp. sweet balsamic vinegar

Directions

1. Set your air fryer toast oven to 370 degrees F and add the oil, onions and 1/2 teaspoon of salt to the pan of your air fryer toast oven. Cook for 2 minutes until golden.
2. Add the chicken drumsticks and sprinkle with the rest of the salt, pepper and chili, then add the thyme, garlic cloves, and lemon zest; add in balsamic vinegar and tomatoes and spread the mixture between the drumsticks.
3. Air roast for about 20 minutes or until done to desire.
4. Serve the creamy chicken over rice, pasta or potatoes or with a side of vegetables.
5. Enjoy!

Nutrition value per serving:

Calories: 329 kcal, Carbs: 13.3 g, Fat: 0.4 g, Protein: 20.8 g.

Scrumptious Turkey Wraps

Prep Time: 15 minutes/ Cook Time 10 minutes/ Serves: 4

Ingredients

- 250g ground turkey
- 1/2 small onion, finely chopped
- 1 garlic clove, minced
- 2 tablespoons extra virgin olive oil
- 1 head lettuce
- 1 teaspoon cumin
- 1/2 tablespoon fresh ginger, sliced
- 2 tablespoons apple cider vinegar
- 2 tablespoons freshly chopped cilantro
- 1 teaspoon freshly ground black pepper
- 1 teaspoon sea salt

Directions

1. Sauté garlic and onion in extra virgin olive oil until fragrant and translucent in your air fryer toast oven pan at 350 degrees F.
2. Add turkey and cook well for 5-8 minutes or until done to desire.
3. Add in the remaining ingredients and continue cooking for 5 minutes more.
4. To serve, ladle a spoonful of turkey mixture onto a lettuce leaf and wrap. Enjoy!

Nutrition value per serving:

Calories: 197 kcal, Carbs: 8.4 g, Fat: 17.9 g, Protein: 13.4 g.

Air Roasted Whole Chicken

Prep Time: 15 minutes/ Cook Time 50 minutes/ Serves: 12

Ingredients

- 1 full chicken, dissected
- 2 tablespoons extra virgin olive oil
- 2 tablespoons chopped garlic
- 2 teaspoons sea salt
- 1 teaspoon pepper
- 1 tablespoons chopped fresh thyme
- 1 tablespoons chopped fresh rosemary

Fruit Compote

- 1 apple, diced
- 1/2 cup red grapes, halved, seeds removed
- 12 dried apricots, sliced
- 16 dried figs, coarsely chopped
- 1/2 cup chopped red onion
- 1/2 cup cider vinegar
- 1/2 cup dry white wine
- 2 teaspoons liquid stevia
- 1/2 teaspoon salt
- 1/2 teaspoon pepper

Directions

1. In a small bowl, stir together thyme, rosemary, garlic, salt and pepper and rub the mixture over the pork.
2. Light your air fryer toast oven and set it to 320°F, place the chicken on the basket and air roast for 10 minutes.
3. Increase the temperature and cook for another 10 minutes, turning the chicken pieces once. Increase the temperature one more time to 400 degrees F and cook for 5 minutes to get a crispy finish.
4. Make Fruit Compote: In a saucepan, combine all ingredients and cook

over medium heat, stirring, for about 25 minutes or until liquid is reduced to a quarter.

5. Once the chicken is cooked, serve hot with a ladle of fruit compote Enjoy!

Nutrition value per serving:

Calories: 511 kcal, Carbs: 15 g, Fat: 36.8 g, Protein: 31.5 g.

CHAPTER 5: VEGAN & VEGETARIAN

Air Fried Vegetables

Ingredients:

- 2 tablespoons extra virgin olive oil
- 1 tablespoon minced garlic
- 1 large shallot, sliced
- 1 cup mushrooms, sliced
- 1 cup broccoli florets
- 1 cup artichoke hearts
- 1 bunch asparagus, sliced into 3-inch pieces
- 1 cup baby peas
- 1 cup cherry tomatoes, halved
- 1/2 teaspoon sea salt

Vinaigrette
- 3 tablespoons white wine vinegar
- 6 tablespoons extra-virgin olive oil
- 1/2 teaspoon sea salt
- 1 teaspoon ground oregano
- handful fresh parsley, chopped

Directions

1. Add oil to the pan of your air fryer toast oven set over medium heat. Stir in garlic and shallots and air fry for about 2 minutes.
2. Stir in mushrooms for about 3 minutes or until golden.
3. Stir in broccoli, artichokes, and asparagus and continue cooking for 3 more minutes. Stir in peas, tomatoes and salt and transfer to the air fryer toast oven and cook for 5-8 more minutes.
4. Prepare vinaigrette: mix together vinegar, oil, salt, oregano and parsley in a bowl until well combined.
5. Serve the air fried vegetable in a serving bowl and drizzle with vinaigrette. Toss to combine and serve.

Nutrition value per serving:

Calories: 293 kcal, Carbs: 14.6 g, Fat: 27 g, Protein: 25 g.

Air Broiled Mushrooms

Prep Time: 10 minutes/ Cook Time 10 minutes/ Serves: 4

Ingredients

- 2 cups shiitake mushrooms
- 1 tablespoon balsamic vinegar
- 1/4 cup extra virgin olive oil
- 1-2 garlic cloves, minced
- A handful of parsley
- 1 teaspoon salt

Directions

1. Rinse the mushroom and pat dry; put in a foil and drizzle with balsamic vinegar and extra virgin olive oil.
2. Sprinkle the mushroom with garlic, parsley, and salt.
3. Broil for about 10 minutes in your air fryer toast oven at 350 degrees F or until tender and cooked through. Serve warm.

Nutrition value per serving:

Calories: 260 kcal, Carbs: 11 g, Fat: 19.1 g, Protein: 22 g.

Hydrated Potato Wedges

Prep Time: 5 minutes/ Cook Time 30 minutes/ Serves: 5

Ingredients

- 2 medium Russet potatoes, diced into wedges
- 1 1/2 tablespoons olive oil
- 1/2 teaspoon chili powder
- 1/2 teaspoon parsley
- 1/2 teaspoon paprika
- 1/8 teaspoon black pepper
- 1/2 teaspoon sea salt

Directions

1. In a large bowl, mix potato wedges, olive oil, chili, parsley, paprika, salt and pepper until the potatoes are well coated.
2. Transfer half of the potatoes to a fryer basket and hydrate for 20 minutes.
3. Repeat with the remaining wedges. Serve hot with chilled orange juice.

Nutrition value per serving:

Calories: 129 kcal, Carbs: 10 g, Fat: 5.3 g, Protein: 2.3 g.

Crispy Baked Tofu

Prep Time: 15 minutes/ Cook Time 20 minutes/ Serves: 4

Ingredients

- 1 cup whole wheat flour
- 1 package (16-ounce) extra firm tofu, chopped into 8 slices
- 3/4 cup raw cashews
- 2 cups pretzel sticks
- 1 tbsp. extra virgin olive oil
- 2 tsp. chili powder
- 1 cup unsweetened almond milk
- 2 tsp. garlic powder
- 2 tsp. onion powder
- 1 tsp. lemon pepper
- 1/4 tsp. black pepper
- 1/2 tsp. sea salt

Directions

1. Preheat your air fryer toast oven to 400 degrees F.
2. Line a baking sheet with baking paper and set aside.
3. In a food processor, pulse together cashews and pretzel sticks until coarsely ground.
4. Combine garlic, onion, chili powder, lemon pepper, and salt in a small bowl.
5. In a large bowl, combine half of the spice mixture and flour.
6. Add almond milk to a separate bowl.
7. In another bowl, combine cashew mixture, salt, pepper and olive oil; mix well.
8. Sprinkle tofu slices with the remaining half of the spice mixture and coat each with the flour and then dip in almond mil; coat with the cashew mixture and bake for about 18 minutes or until golden brown.
9. Serve the baked tofu with favorite vegan salad.

Nutrition value per serving:

Calories: 332 kcal, Carbs: 23.3 g, Fat: 8.8 g, Protein: 12.9 g.

Spiced Tempeh

Prep Time: 15 minutes/ Cook Time 20 minutes/ Serves: 4

Ingredients

Tempeh Bits:
- 1/4 cup vegetable oil
- 8 oz. tempeh
- 1 tsp. lemon pepper
- 1 tsp. chili powder
- 2 tsp. sweet paprika
- 2 tsp. garlic powder
- 2 tsp. onion powder
- 1/4 tsp. sea salt
- 1/8 tsp. cayenne pepper or more to taste

Salad:
- 15.5 oz. can chickpeas
- 1 lb. chopped kale
- 1 cup shredded carrots
- 2 tbsp. sesame seeds, toasted

Dressing:
- 1 tbsp. fresh grated ginger
- 2 tbsp. toasted sesame oil
- 1/4 cup low sodium soy sauce
- 1/3 cup seasoned rice vinegar

Directions

1. Blanch kale in a pot of salted boiling water for about 30 seconds and immediately run under cold water; drain and squeeze out excess water. Set aside.
2. Preheat your air fryer toast oven to 425 degrees F.
3. In a small bowl, combine all the spices for tempeh.

4. Add oil to a separate bowl. Slice tempeh into thin pieces.
5. Dip each tempeh slice into the oil and arrange them on a paper-lined baking sheet; generously sprinkle with the spices until well covered and bake for about 20 minutes or until crispy and golden brown then remove from air fryer toast oven. In a large bowl, combine all the salad ingredients and set aside.
6. In a jar, combine all the dressing ingredients; close and shake until well blended; pour the dressing over salad and toss to coat well.
7. Crumble the crispy tempeh on top of the salad to serve. Enjoy!

Nutrition value per serving:

Calories: 308 kcal, Carbs: 19.2 g, Fat: 7.3 g, Protein: 9.8 g.

Steamed Broccoli

Prep Time: 8 minutes/ Cook Time 3 minutes/ Serves: 2

Ingredients

- 1 pound broccoli florets
- 1-1/2 cups water
- Salt and pepper to taste
- I tsp. extra virgin olive oil

Directions

1. Add water to the bottom of your air fryer toast oven and set the basket on top.
2. Toss the broccoli florets with, salt pepper and olive oil until evenly combined then transfer to the basket of your air fryer toast oven.
3. Select keep warm for 10 minutes.
4. Remove the basket and serve the broccoli.

Nutrition value per serving:

Calories: 160 kcal, Carbs: 6.1 g, Fat: 12 g, Protein: 13 g.

Air Fried Brussel Sprouts

Prep Time: 10 minutes/ Cook Time 10 minutes/ Serves: 4

Ingredients

- 2 pound Brussels sprouts, halved
- 1 tbsp. chopped almonds
- 1 tbsp. rice vinegar
- 2 tbsp. sriracha sauce
- 1/4 cup gluten free soy sauce
- 2 tbsp. sesame oil
- 1/2 tbsp. cayenne pepper
- 1 tbsp. smoked paprika
- 1 tsp. onion powder
- 2 tsp. garlic powder
- 1 tsp. red pepper flakes
- Salt and pepper

Directions

1. Preheat your air fryer toast oven to 370 degrees F.
2. Meanwhile place your air fryer toast oven's pan on medium heat and cook the almonds for 3 minutes then add in all the remaining ingredients.
3. Place the pan in the air fryer toast oven and air fry for 8-10 minutes or until done to desire.
4. Serve hot over a bed of steamed rice.
5. Enjoy!

Nutrition value per serving:

Calories: 216 kcal, Carbs: 8.8 g, Fat: 18 g, Protein: 18g.

Hydrated Kale Chips

Prep Time: 5 minutes/ Cook Time 5 minutes/ Serves: 2

Ingredients

- 4 cups loosely packed kale, stemmed
- 2 teaspoons ranch Seasoning
- 2 tablespoons olive oil
- 1 tablespoon nutritional yeast
- 1/4 teaspoon salt

Directions

1. In a bowl, toss together kale pieces, oil, nutritional yeast, ranch seasoning, and salt until well coated.
2. Transfer to a fryer basket and hydrate for 15 minutes, shaking halfway through cooking.
3. Serve right away!

Nutrition value per serving:

Calories: 103 kcal, Carbs: 8.2 g, Fat: 7.1 g, Protein: 3.2 g.

CHAPTER 6: SOUPS, STEWS & BROTHS

Chicken and Veggie Soup

Prep Time: 10 minutes/ Cook Time 30 minutes/ Serves: 1

Ingredients

- 1 teaspoon extra-virgin olive oil
- 100 grams chicken
- 1 clove garlic, minced
- 1 tablespoon chopped red onion
- 1/2 lemon with rind
- 1 stalk lemongrass
- 1/4 teaspoon thyme
- Pinch of cayenne pepper
- Pinch of salt & pepper
- 2 cups chicken broth
- 1/4 cup fresh lemon juice
- 2 cups chopped spinach

Directions

1. In your air fryer, air roast chicken in olive oil for 6 minutes at 350 degrees F, turning the chicken halfway through cook time.
2. Transfer to a saucepan and stir in garlic, onion, herbs, spices, broth, lemon juice and lemon rind and simmer for about 25 minutes, adding spinach during the last 5 minutes.
3. Serve hot.

Nutrition value per serving:

Calories: 197 kcal, Carbs: 7.8 g, Fat: 15 g, Protein: 17 g.

Air Roasted Roots Soup

Prep Time: 10 minutes/ Cook Time 1 hour/ Serves: 5

Ingredients

- 2 tablespoons extra virgin olive oil
- 2 red onions, quartered
- 2 red peppers, deseeded, chopped
- 3 tomatoes, halved
- 3 carrots, peeled, diced
- 2 sweet potatoes, peeled, diced
- 2 cans light coconut milk
- 1 teaspoon ground cumin
- 1 tablespoon smoked paprika, plus extra for garnish
- 2 inches fresh root ginger, peeled, minced
- 1 bay leaf
- Salt and black pepper
- Chopped coriander to garnish
- Lime wedges

Directions

1. Preheat oven your air fryer toast oven to 400°F.
2. In you air fryer toast oven's pan, mix all the veggies and oil and air roast in the air fryer toast oven for about 40 minutes or until cooked.
3. Remove from air fryer toast oven.
4. Chop the roasted vegetables and place them in a saucepan; add the remaining ingredients and stir to mix well; season with salt and bring the mixture to a gentle boil in a sauce pan and then simmer for about 20 minutes.
5. Divide the soup among six serving bowls and sprinkle each with coriander, black pepper and smoked paprika.
6. Garnish with lime wedges and enjoy!

Nutrition value per serving:

Calories: 390 kcal, Carbs: 11 g, Fat: 22 g, Protein: 19 g.

CHAPTER 7: DESSERTS AND SNACKS

Air Baked Cheesecake

Prep Time: 20 minutes/ Cook Time 20 minutes/ Serves: 8-12

Ingredients

Crust

- 1/2 cup dates, chopped, soaked in water for at least 15 min., soaking liquid reserved
- 1/2 cup walnuts
- 1 cup quick oats

Filling

- 1/2 cup vanilla almond milk
- 1/4 cup coconut palm sugar
- 1/2 cup coconut flour
- 1 cup cashews, soaked in water for at least 2 hours
- 1 tsp. vanilla extract
- 2 tbsp. lemon juice
- 1 to 2 tsp. grated lemon zest
- 1/2 cup fresh berries or 6 figs, sliced
- 1 tbsp. arrowroot powder

Directions

1. Make the crust: in a food processor, process together all the crust ingredients until smooth and press the mixture into the bottom of a spring form pan.
2. Make the filling: add cashews along with soaking liquid to a blender and process until very smooth; add milk, palm sugar, coconut flour, lemon juice, lemon zest, and vanilla and blend until well combined;

add arrowroot and continue blending until mixed and pour into the crust. Smooth the top and cover the spring form pan with foil.
3. Place the pan in your air fry toaster oven and bake at 375 degrees F for 20 minutes.
4. Carefully remove the pan from the fryer and remove the foil; let the cake cool completely and top with fruit to serve.

Nutrition value per serving:

Calories: 423 kcal, Carbs: 33.5 g, Fat: 3.1 g, Protein: 1.2 g.

Air Roasted Nuts

Prep Time: 10 minutes/ Cook Time 20 minutes/ Serves: 8

Ingredients

- 1 cup raw peanuts
- 1/2 teaspoon cayenne pepper
- 3 teaspoons seafood seasoning
- 2 tablespoons olive oil
- salt

Directions

1. Preheat your air fryer toast oven to 320° F.
2. In a bowl, whisk together cayenne pepper, olive oil, and seafood seasoning; stir in peanuts until well coated.
3. Transfer to the fryer basket and air roast for 10 minutes; toss well and then cook for another 10 minutes.
4. Transfer the peanuts to a dish and season with salt. Let cool before serving.

Nutrition value per serving:

Calories: 193 kcal, Carbs: 4.9 g, Fat: 17.4 g, Protein: 7.4 g.

Air Fried White Corn

Prep Time: 10 minutes/ Cook Time 40 minutes/ Serves: 8

Ingredients

- 2 cups giant white corn
- 3 tablespoons olive oil
- 1-1/2 teaspoons sea salt

Directions

1. Soak the corn in a bowl of water for at least 8 hours or overnight; drain and spread in a single layer on a baking tray; pat dry with paper towels.
2. Preheat your air fryer toast oven to 400° F.
3. In a bowl, mix corn, olive oil and salt and toss to coat well.
4. Air fry corn in batches in the preheated air fryer toast oven for 20 minutes, shaking the basket halfway through cooking.
5. Let the corn cool for at least 20 minutes or until crisp.

Nutrition value per serving:

Calories: 225 kcal, Carbs: 35.8g, Fat: 7.4 g, Protein: 5.9 g.

Fruit Cake

Prep Time: 5 minutes/ Cook Time 45 minutes/ Serves: 4-6

Ingredients

Dry Ingredients
- 1/8 teaspoon sea salt
- 1/2 teaspoon baking powder
- 1/2 teaspoon baking soda
- 1/2 teaspoon ground cardamom
- 1-1/4 cup whole wheat flour

Wet Ingredients
- 2 tablespoons coconut oil
- 1/2 cup unsweetened nondairy milk
- 2 tablespoons ground flax seeds
- 1/4 cup agave
- 1-1/2 cups water

Mix-Ins
- 1/2 cup chopped cranberries
- 1 cup chopped pear

Directions

1. Grease a Bundt pan; set aside.
2. In a mixing, mix all dry ingredients together. In another bowl, combine together the wet ingredients; whisk the wet ingredients into the dry until smooth.
3. Fold in the add-ins and spread the mixture into the pan; cover with foil.
4. Place pan in your air fryer toast oven and add water in the bottom and bake at 370 degrees F for 35 minutes.
5. When done, use a toothpick to check for doneness. Of it comes out clean, then the cake is ready, if not, bake for 5-10 more minutes, checking frequently to avoid burning.
6. Remove the cake and let stand for 10 minutes before transferring from the pan.
7. Enjoy!

Nutrition value per serving:

Calories: 309 kcal, Carbs: 14.7 g, Fat: 27 g, Protein: 22.6 g.

Hydrated Apples

Prep Time: 5 minutes/ Cook Time 15 minutes/ Serves: 6

Ingredients

- 6 apples, cored
- 1 teaspoon cinnamon powder
- 1/2 cup sugar
- 1 cup red wine
- 1/4 cup raisins

Directions

1. Add apples to your air fryer toast oven's pan and then add wine, cinnamon powder, sugar and raisins.
2. Hydrate for 20 minutes and remove from air fry toaster oven.
3. Serve the apples in small serving bowls drizzled with lots of cooking juices.
4. Enjoy!

Nutrition value per serving:

Calories: 229 kcal, Carbs: 53.3 g, Fat: 0.4 g, Protein: 0.8 g.

Nutty Slice

Prep Time: 10 minutes/ Cook Time 30 minutes/ Serves: 4

Ingredients:

- 4 cups fresh or frozen mixed berries
- 1 cup almond meal
- 1/2 cup almond butter
- 1 cup oven roasted walnuts, sunflower seeds, pistachios.
- 1/2 tsp. ground cinnamon

Directions

1. Preheat air fryer toast oven to 375 degrees F.
2. Crush the nuts using a mortar and pestle.
3. In a bowl, combine the nut mix, almond meal, cinnamon and ghee and combine well.
4. In a pie dish, spread half the nut mixture over the bottom of the dish, then top with the berries and finish with the rest of the nut mixture.
5. Bake for 30 minutes. Slice and serve warm with natural vanilla yogurt.
6. Yum!

Nutrition value per serving:

Calories: 278 kcal, Carbs: 10.3 g, Fat: 15.7 g, Protein: 13.8 g.

Energy Brownies

Prep Time: 10 minutes/ Cook Time 35 minutes/ Serves: 10

Ingredients

- 1-1/2 cups unsweetened shredded coconut
- 1/2 cup dried cranberries
- 1/2 cup golden flax meal
- 1/2 cup coconut butter
- 1 cup hemp seeds
- A good pinch of sea salt

Directions

1. Combine the cranberries, flax, and hemp seeds in the bowl of your food processor and pulse until well-ground.
2. Add the shredded coconut, coconut butter, stevia, and salt and pulse until it forms thick dough.
3. Transfer the dough to a baking dish and bake for 10 minutes in your air fryer toast oven at 370 degrees F, then remove from air fryer toast oven.
4. Let cool completely, then chill in the fridge to firm up. Slice it into bars and enjoy!

Nutrition value per serving:

Calories: 314 kcal, Carbs: 19.8 g, Fat: 10.1 g, Protein: 7.8 g.

Air Fry Toaster Oven Bars

Prep Time: 5 minutes/ Cook Time 25 minutes/ Serves: 4

Ingredients

- 1 cup chopped chocolate
- 2 ripe avocados
- 1 tsp. raw honey
- 2 tsp. vanilla extract
- 4 eggs
- 1 cup ground almonds
- 1/2 cup cocoa powder
- 1/4 tsp. salt

Directions

1. Prepare an 8-inch baking pan by lining it with foil and then coating with non-stick cooking spray.
2. Add chocolate to a bowl and place over a large saucepan of boiling water.
3. Stir until chocolate is melted. Remove from heat and let cool.
4. Meanwhile, prepare the batter: in a bowl, mash the avocados; add honey and stir to combine.
5. Whisk in vanilla extract and eggs until well blended. Gradually whisk in the chocolate until well incorporated.
6. Stir in ground almonds, cocoa powder, and salt until well blended.
7. Transfer the batter to the prepared baking pan and cover with a paper towel and then with aluminum foil.
8. Place the pan in your air fryer toast oven and bake at 375 degrees F for 30 minutes or until done to desire.
9. Let cool completely before cutting into squares. These brownies are best served chilled.

Nutrition value per serving:

Calories: 512 kcal, Carbs: 31.2 g, Fat: 12.3 g, Protein: 14.4 g.

CHAPTER 8: BEANS AND EGGS

Air Fried Beans

Prep Time: 5 minutes/ Cook Time 30 minutes/ Serves: 6

Ingredients

- 2 pounds dried pinto beans, sorted and soaked, rinsed
- 5 garlic cloves, roughly chopped
- 1-1/2 cups chopped onion
- 3 tablespoons vegetable shortening
- 1-1/2 teaspoons ground cumin
- 2 teaspoons dried oregano
- 1 jalapeno, seeded and chopped
- 4 cups vegetable broth
- 1-2 teaspoons sea salt
- 4 cups water
- 1/2 teaspoon ground black pepper

Directions

1. Mix all the ingredients in a pan that can fit in your air fryer toaster basket and cook on bake for 30 minutes.
2. Press the keep warm button for 10 minutes.
3. Stir in sea salt and transfer the mixture to a blender; blend to your desired consistency and serve.

Nutritional value per Serving:

Calories: 203; Fat: 1.6 g; Carbs: 12.3 g; Protein: 5.9 g;

Egg and Spinach Scramble

Prep Time: 8 minutes/ Cook Time 30 minutes/ Serves: 1

Ingredients

- 3 egg whites
- 1 cup (packed) spinach
- 1 onion, chopped
- 2 tbsp. extra virgin olive oil
- 1/2 tsp. onion powder
- 1/2 tsp. garlic powder
- 1 tsp. turmeric powder
- Ground pepper to taste

Directions

1. Preheat your air fry toaster oven to 350 F.
2. Beat the egg whites and oil in a large bowl. Add in the fresh ingredients and mix until well combined then set the bowl aside.
3. Lightly grease your foodi air fry toaster oven's frying pan and transfer the egg mixture into the pan.
4. Set your air fry toaster oven to bake setting for about 10 minutes or until done to desire.
5. Serve hot.

Nutrition value per serving:

Calories: 285 kcal, Carbs: 12.3 g, Fat: 21.6 g, Protein: 13 g.

Hydrated Green Beans

Prep Time: 10 minutes/ Cook Time 20 minutes/ Serves: 4

Ingredients

- 12 ounces trimmed fresh green beans
- 1 teaspoon rice wine vinegar
- 1 teaspoon soy sauce
- 1 tablespoon sesame oil
- 1/2 teaspoon red pepper flakes
- 1 clove garlic, minced

Directions

1. Add the green beans to a large bowl; in a small bowl, mix together rice wine vinegar, soy sauce, sesame oil, red pepper flakes, and garlic until well combined; pour over the green beans and toss to coat well.
2. Place green beans in a bowl. Let marinate for at least 5 minutes and then transfer half to a fryer basket.
3. Hydrate for 20 minutes, shaking the basket halfway through cooking. Repeat with the remaining green beans.

Nutrition value per serving:

Calories: 59 kcal, Carbs: 6.6 g, Fat: 3.6 g, Protein: 1.7 g.

Egg and Mushroom Frittata

Prep Time: 8 minutes/ Cook Time 12 minutes/ Serves: 2

Ingredients

- 4 egg whites
- 1/3 cup mushrooms, sliced
- 1 large tomato, sliced
- 1/4 cup finely chopped chives
- 2 tbsp. milk
- Salt and freshly ground black pepper to taste

Directions

1. Beat the egg whites and milk in a large bowl. Add in the fresh ingredients and mix until well combined then set the bowl aside.
2. Lightly grease your air fryer toast oven's frying pan and transfer the egg mixture into the pan.
3. Set on baking at 320 degrees for 12 minutes or until done to your desire.

Nutrition value per serving:

Calories: 360 kcal, Carbs: 10.8 g, Fat: 28.6 g, Protein: 4.6 g.

Air Baked Omelet

Prep Time: 10 minutes/ Cook Time 10 minutes/ Serves: 2

Ingredients

- 3 large eggs
- 100g ham, cut into small pieces
- 1/4 cup milk
- 3/4 cup mixed vegetables (white mushrooms, green onions, red pepper)
- 1/4 cup mixed cheddar and mozzarella cheese
- 1 tsp. freshly chopped mixed herbs (cilantro and chives)
- Salt and freshly ground pepper to taste

Directions

1. Combine the eggs and milk in a medium bowl then add in the remaining ingredients apart from the cheese and mixed herbs and beat well using a fork.
2. Pour the egg mix into an evenly greased pan then place it in the basket of your air fryer.
3. Bake for roughly 10 minutes at 350 degrees F or until done to desire.
4. Sprinkle the cheese and mixed herbs on the omelet halfway through cook time.
5. Gently loosen the omelet from the sides of the pan using a spatula.
6. Serve hot!

Nutrition value per serving:

Calories: 411 kcal, Carbs: 14 g, Fat: 39.3 g, Protein: 28 g.

Air Fryer Cooked Bean Dish

Yield: 4-6 Servings/ Total Time: 20 Minutes/ Prep Time: 10 Minutes/ Cook Time: 10 Minutes

Ingredients

- 280g canned sweet corn, do not drain
- 750g diced tomato with the juices
- 100g canned white kidney beans, do not drain
- 100g canned navy beans, do not drain
- 200g canned black-eyed peas, do not drain
- 1 purple onion, chopped
- 1 green pepper, diced
- 3 cloves garlic, finely chopped
- 1/4 cup mild chili powder
- 1/2 tbsp. ground cumin

Directions

1. Mix the peas, beans, tomatoes, corn, onion, pepper, garlic, cumin and chili powder in a pan that fits in your air fryer toaster basket and stir to combine well.
2. Set on bake at 350 degrees for 20 minutes.
3. Set on keep warm for 5 minutes and then remove from oven. Serve right away.

Nutritional value per Serving:

Calories: 485; Fat: 3 g; Carbs: 99.6 g; Protein: 18.2 g;

Bacon Omelet

Prep Time: 10 minutes/ Cook Time 10 minutes/ Serves: 2

Ingredients

- 3 large eggs
- 100g bacon, cut into small pieces
- 1/4 cup milk
- 3/4 cup mixed vegetables (mushrooms, scallions, bell pepper)
- 1/4 cup mixed cheddar and mozzarella cheese
- 1 tsp. mixed herbs
- Salt and freshly ground pepper to taste

Directions

1. Combine the eggs and milk in a medium bowl then add in the remaining ingredients apart from the cheese and mixed herbs and beat well using a fork.
2. Pour the egg mix into an evenly greased pan then place it in the basket of your air fryer toast oven.
3. Air fry for roughly 10 minutes at 350 degrees F or until done to desire.
4. Sprinkle the cheese and mixed herbs on the omelet halfway through cook time.
5. Gently loosen the omelet from the sides of the pan using a spatula.
6. Serve hot!

Nutrition value per serving:

Calories: 278 kcal, Carbs: 1.3 g, Fat: 4.6 g, Protein: 24.1 g.

Air Fryer Baked Beans

Prep Time: 10 minutes/ Cook Time 25 minutes/ Serves: 4-6

Ingredients

- 1 cup shiitake mushrooms
- 1 + 1/2 cups dry cannellini beans
- 2 cloves of garlic, diced
- 1 medium carrot, diced
- 1/2 long red chili diced
- 1 large brown onion, diced
- 2 tablespoons olive oil
- 1 cup warm water
- 1/4 teaspoon sea salt
- 2 cups chopped tomatoes
- 1 tablespoon Tamari sauce
- 2 tablespoons brown sugar
- 1 tablespoon ketchup
- 1/2 teaspoon allspice powder
- 1/2 teaspoon regular paprika
- 1 onion stock cube
- 1 teaspoon smoked paprika
- 2 bay leaves

Directions

1. Soak dried beans in a bowl of salted water for at least 8 hours; drain and rinse before using.
2. Soak mushrooms for about 20 minutes.
3. Combine all ingredients in a pan that fits in an air fry toaster oven basket and place in the oven. Cook on bake for 12 minutes and then press the keep warm button for 10 minutes.
4. Serve over rice or toast.

Nutritional value per Serving:

Calories: 341; Fat: 9.6 g; Carbs: 17.9 g; Protein: 5.9 g;

Conclusion

Congratulations for coming to the end of this Ninja Foodi Digital Air Fryer Oven Cookbook. By now you have all the information regarding this amazing air fryer oven and if you don't have it yet, you now have all the information you need to make your purchase. If you already have well, time to put on your apron and cook our tasty and simple recipes that will leave your family and friends singing your praises.

Take your time as you try our recipes and remember to enjoy the experience of this wonder cooking air fryer oven!

Share your experience with the SharkNinja team and remember to recommend it to your family and friends. All the best as you elevate your cooking experience!

CPSIA information can be obtained
at www.ICGtesting.com
Printed in the USA
LVHW100055200221
679372LV00002B/66

9 781954 294905